T0195710

THE CONSTITUTION OF
SINT MAARTEN

When It is Time to Vote

HENSLEY G. A. PLANTIJN

WESTBOW
PRESS®
A DIVISION OF THOMAS NELSON
& ZONDERVAN

WestBow Press books may be ordered through booksellers or by contacting:

WestBow Press
A Division of Thomas Nelson & Zondervan
1663 Liberty Drive
Bloomington, IN 47403
www.westbowpress.com
1 (866) 928-1240

ISBN: 978-1-9736-8935-5 (sc)
ISBN: 978-1-9736-8937-9 (hc)
ISBN: 978-1-9736-8936-2 (e)

Library of Congress Control Number: 2020906512

Print information available on the last page.

WestBow Press rev. date: 04/09/2020

The knowledge of the Constitution by the people of Sint Maarten will determine the level of development of their country.

—Hensley G. A. Plantijn

CONTENTS

INTRODUCTION

On June 23, 2000, a referendum was held among the population of Sint Maarten regarding the political future of the island. As a result, the majority of the population of Sint Maarten chose to become a country within the Kingdom of the Netherlands. Becoming a country obviously meant that Sint Maarten had to leave the constellation of the Netherlands Antilles.

The result of the mentioned referendum, the wish of the people of Sint Maarten, was presented during the initial Round Table Conference (RTC) of the Kingdom of the Netherlands in November 2005. All the partners in the kingdom agreed that Sint Maarten would become a country within the Kingdom of the Netherlands. To become a country within the Kingdom of the Netherlands, the first law needed in Sint Maarten was a state regulation or a constitution.

The following is mentioned in the explanatory memorandum of the constitution:

This draft Constitution formulates and guarantees the fundamental rights of the citizens and covers the position of the main institutions of the country of Sint Maarten. This makes it the main reference for the constitutional law of the forthcoming country of Sint Maarten. The Constitution of the country of Sint Maarten is based on the principles of a democratic state under the rule of law. A distinguishing feature of the concept of a state under the rule of law is the legality principle, meaning that all government action should be based on statutory grounds and furthermore, that the national ordinances should comply with certain quality requirements. This promotes legal certainty and legal equality. The democracy principle relates to the method of political decision-making, namely through the participation of all citizens. In a democratic state under the rule of law, the majority decides, but protection and respect for the minorities is also essential. The draft assumes a representative parliamentary system, with opportunities for more direct participation by means including a consultative referendum, …

Another feature of the concept of a democratic state under the rule of law is the "trias politica." A spread of powers over different offices is an important means of countering abuse of government power. A key issue in that regard is that the three government functions of legislation, administration and administration of justice are assigned to different offices. The aim is to further prevent abuse through checks and balances between the different offices.

Finally, it is important to note in connection with the checks and balances that the court will be assigned the power to assess legislation in terms of, in principle, the entire Constitution. This constitutional assessment sharply increases the control of the judiciary over the legislature … A final feature of the democratic state under the rule of law concerns the recognition of the fundamental rights of citizens …

Three objectives in particular took priority in the design of this draft Constitution. Firstly, a strengthening of the fundamental rights, secondly, a strengthening of representation and the democratic principle and thirdly, the promotion of the binding of political processes by constitutional principles.

It should be mentioned that entering the status of country, Sint Maarten has established a very transparent election process. Nowhere in the Kingdom of the Netherlands is an institution similar to the Electoral Council, with all its tasks and authority, established. All the necessary obligations of the political parties participating in an election are published. The financing of the political parties and the candidates should be reported. The voter can follow all actions of the political parties as prescribed by the laws. The best information the voter has access to is the articles of incorporation of the political party. This is established by notarial deed. In here the political party needs to establish its objectives and how they will be achieved. The steps to achieve the objectives should then be presented in the party manifesto.

The conclusion is that at the birth of the country of Sint Maarten, the lawmakers made sure that the voter has access to all the necessary information of a political party participating in the elections. Therefore, the voter, should first select a political party. If the political party is in full compliance with the laws and regulations, the voter then needs to choose between the several manifestos and choose the one that according to the voter will be beneficial for the development of the country—Sint Maarten. The voter can then vote for a candidate of his preference on the political party he just selected.

CHAPTER 1

A Short History of the Parliament of Sint Maarten

The Parliament of Sint Maarten

The will of the people is the foundation of the government's authority. This will is expressed by a people's representation, the Parliament. The members of Parliament are selected by direct, regular, free, and confidential elections. This is regulated in article 47 of the Constitution.

Furthermore, article 49 regulates that to be eligible for membership of Parliament, a person must be a resident of Sint Maarten, a Dutch national who is at least eighteen years old and who has not been disqualified from voting.

Based on article 44, Parliament represents the entire population.

In constitutional terms, this provision not only expresses that Parliament plays a key role in the uniting of Sint Maarten but also that the members of Parliament may not conduct themselves as representatives of local or regional interests or particular interests based on other criteria, but represent the general interest of the entire population of Sint Maarten.

This provision also means that, strictly speaking, the representation of the people of Sint Maarten bears no relationship to the number of voters for Parliament or to the electoral system on the basis of which the members are elected. This relationship is regulated in article 46 of the Constitution.

Article 45 further regulates the composition of Parliament. The explanatory memorandum mentions that when the island territory of Aruba gained the status of a constituent country of the kingdom on January 1, 1986, it was regulated in the Constitution of Aruba that its Parliament would consist of twenty-one members, the same number of members as that of the Aruban Island Council at the time. The same was true of the parliament of the new constituent country of Curaçao.

Following this line of reasoning, the Parliament of Sint Maarten could be made up of the same number of members as the former Island Council of Sint Maarten (i.e., eleven). However, it was considered that a good, broadly based, and well-equipped parliamentary system, in which the checks and balances can be realized to the fullest, is necessary to perform the key tasks for parliamentary democracy. For this reason, a Parliament of fifteen members was chosen instead of the eleven members that made up the Island Council.

It is important to mention that a total membership of fifteen is also more likely to do justice to the diversity in the population of Sint Maarten. Because the quota with fifteen members will be smaller than with eleven members, smaller parties will have a greater chance of representation in Parliament.

There is also a relationship between the size of the population and the size of the Parliament. Considering the history of the island territory, the possibility of an increase in population is not inconceivable. According to the population register, the population of the island territory of Sint Maarten consisted of 53,653 registered inhabitants in June 2010.

In connection with this, it was proposed that Parliament will consist of fifteen members if the population of Sint Maarten is sixty thousand or less, seventeen members if the population is more than sixty thousand but no more than seventy thousand, nineteen members if the population is more than seventy thousand but no more than eighty thousand, and twenty-one members if the population exceeds eighty thousand.

Please note that in accordance with paragraph 2 of mentioned article 45, an increase or reduction in the number of members of Parliament arising from a change in the population of the country first takes effect on the next regular election of Parliament.

In accordance with article 46, the duration of Parliament shall be four years. And the sessions commence on the second Tuesday of September or at an earlier date to be laid down by national ordinance. The parliamentary year is related to the budget cycle that the government should maintain in the implementation of the budget adopted by Parliament.

Paragraph 3 of article 46 regulates that the parliamentary year is opened by the president of Parliament. Paragraph 4 regulates that during this special meeting of Parliament, the governor explains the government's policy for the upcoming period.

It is further regulated that after this special meeting, discussions of the draft budget with the individual ministers will commence. These discussions lead to the enactment of the budget for the following year of office.

Finally, because the operation of Parliament entails an increase in the tasks for the members in comparison with the operation of the Island Council, membership of Parliament will constitute a full-time job for the members. The provisions for the members will be appropriate for full-time work.

Political Crisis

Since the birth of the country of Sint Maarten, on October 10, 2010, the constellation of the Parliament of Sint Maarten has changed multiple times.

The first Parliament of Sint Maarten was based on article III of the Constitution of Sint Maarten. Based on this article, the members of the Island Council of Sint Maarten who were in office on October 10, 2010, were automatically established as (the first) members of the Parliament of Sint Maarten.

The first elections for the country of Sint Maarten were held in September 2014.

Those elections were in accordance with article 46 of the Constitution, which mentions that the duration of parliament is four years.

The next election was in September 2016—obviously, within less than the four years mentioned by article 46. However, based on article 59 of the Constitution, the government has the authority to dissolve Parliament and simultaneously call for new (snap) elections. That is what happened. After a motion of nonconfidence was presented to the sitting government, the government bounced back and dissolved the Parliament and called for new elections by national decree with reference number LB-15/0992, dated October 29, 2015.[1]

It is interesting that during the interim period of a new government, the mentioned national decree was adjusted, by a new decree dated December 14, 2015, with reference number LB-15/1110, changing the date of the elections from February 9, 2016, to September 26, 2016.

The next political crisis was in 2017. The situation was almost the same: The government received a motion of nonconfidence by Parliament and decided by national

---

[1] This national ordinance replaced the national ordinance of October 28, 2015, with reference number LB-15/0951.

decree, dated November 2, 2017, with reference number LB-17/0619, to dissolve Parliament and call for new elections.

The latest political crisis was in 2019, with the government again losing a majority (followed by a motion of nonconfidence) in Parliament, and still calling for new elections. In this case, the government had to adjust the previous national decree, dated September 23, 2019, with reference number LB-19/0642, by the national decree of October 3, 2019, with reference number LB-19/0675.

One of the reasons was that the members of the Central Voting Bureau resigned, reasoning that the national decree of September 23, 2019, was, among others, an infringement on the passive election rights of the citizens of Sint Maarten to participate in the elections, as mentioned in the Constitution.

Although there where heated discussions on the timing and reasons for the mentioned elections in 2016, 2018, and now planned for 2020, one should not forget that free, transparent, and secret elections are the cornerstones of democracy, and that article 59 of the Constitution, the authority of the government to dissolve Parliament and call for new elections, is also part of the system of checks and balances in our parliamentary system.[2] [3]

Therefore, as electorate, we need to be aware of the relevant laws and regulations regulating the elections and functioning of Parliament.

Being a representative parliamentary system, the electorate has the power to determine the constellation of Parliament. The role of the voter in determining the outcome of the elections and by extension who is going to be his or her representative to do the checks and balances of the functioning of government is detrimental for the function of this representative and legislative body.

---

[2] Still, one of the most interesting questions asked is if government is still authorized to dissolve Parliament, after receiving a motion of nonconfidence. This will be a subject to be discussed in another book.

[3] It is, however, obvious that there is a discrepancy between the execution of article 59 of the Constitution and the current regulations in, among others, the Election Ordinance. This will be discussed at the end of this book.

CHAPTER 2

Maintaining Transparency in the Elections

The National Ordinance on the Registration and Finances of Political Parties

In order to achieve balanced and responsible progress of elections, Sint Maarten chose to establish the National Ordinance on the registration and finances of political parties. The legal basis for this national ordinance is article 55 paragraph 2 of the Constitution of Sint Maarten.

The Objectives

According to the explanatory memorandum on the mentioned National Ordinance, this national ordinance has two objectives.

The first is to promote a transparent and democratic structure of political parties. Through the proposed introduction of the association form, political parties are assigned the constitutional function in the legislation that they have long held in practice. As a result, it is possible to impose legal rules regarding political parties that can ensure that the design and functioning of these organizations, which are so important for parliamentary democracy, have a proper legal structure that is transparent for the public and is democratic.

It is important to note that an association has members who contribute to the policy of the association in a democratic manner, by voting.

The second is the promotion of the integrity of political parties, the prevention of (the appearance of) conflicts of interest and the promotion of a balanced and clean political process.

Excessively high donations to candidates of parties, in particular, entail a risk of a conflict of interest. For that reason, the prohibition of excessively high donations is proposed. In this way, balanced progress of elections is also promoted, as the funds that parties may receive for their election campaigns are standardized.

The Electoral Council

The institution that needs to assure that the two objectives as mentioned are adhered to is called the Electoral Council. Article 3 in the mentioned National Ordinance establishes the Electoral Council.

This council functions independently of Parliament and the government and is responsible for the tasks assigned to it by or pursuant to the mentioned National Ordinance. It is comprised of three members, including a chairman and a substitute chairman. In addition, there are two substitute members.

The chairman, the substitute chairman, the members, and the substitute members are appointed by national decree on the nomination of the Appointments Committee, based on expertise and experience.

They are appointed for a term of seven years and may be reappointed for one more term.

Registering of the Political Parties

One of the important tasks of the Electoral Council is the registration of the political parties. Namely, in accordance with article 14 of the mentioned National Ordinance, a political party wishing to take part in the elections for Parliament must be registered by the Electoral Council in accordance with the rules stipulated in the National Ordinance. For this, the Electoral Council maintains a register of political parties and of references to political parties, including the names of authorized representatives and alternate authorized representatives of the parties.

In order to be registered by the Electoral Council a political party must be established by notarized deed containing the articles of the association.

The articles of association shall contain at least provisions concerning:

a. the name of the political party;
b. the objective of the political party;
c. the names and the towns of residence of the senior managers and the other officials required by law or by the articles of association;
d. the obligations of the members to the party, or the way in which such obligations can be imposed;
e. the way in which membership is obtained and terminated;
f. the method for convening the general meeting;
g. the powers of the general meeting;

h. the method of appointment and dismissal of the managers;

i. the regulations for representative authorization;

j. the financial resources and their management;

k. a restriction on membership authorized to vote to persons who are authorized to vote in elections for members of Parliament;

l. the obligation to publish a political program in good time before the elections;

m. the procedure for drawing up lists of candidates for the parliamentary elections;

n. the power to amend the articles of association;

o. the dissolution of the association;

p. the beneficiary of any surplus following settlement in the event of the dissolution of the association, and the way that beneficiary shall be determined.

An application for registration must be submitted to the Electoral Council in writing.

The following shall be submitted with the application for registration:

a. A copy of the notarized deed containing the articles of association

b. A declaration from the political party, containing the appointment of its authorized representative and alternate representative to the Electoral Council, which applies until the declaration is replaced

Please note that an application for registration submitted less than six weeks prior to the nomination date shall not be processed for the next election.

The political party's authorized representative and alternate representative to the Electoral Council must be entitled to vote in parliamentary elections.

An authorized representative or alternate representative may act as such for one political party only.

The authorized representative may act as an observer at meetings of the Electoral Council at which the registration of the relevant political party and its finances are discussed and at which decisions on this are taken.

The Electoral Council decides on a complete application within three weeks of its receipt. If the application or accompanying documents require improvement, instead of giving its decision on the application, the Electoral Council shall grant the applicant an opportunity to improve the application or the accompanying documents within one week of notification thereof. In that case, the council shall issue a decision within three weeks of the receipt of the additions or improvements.

The Electoral Council shall reject an application for registration if the requirements of this national ordinance are not met.

The Application

An application for the registration of a political party includes an application for registration of the reference that shall be placed above the lists of candidates to be submitted by the political party.

The application can also be rejected, if the reference:

a. contains more than fifteen letters or other characters;
b. is fully or primarily consistent with a reference of another political party that is already registered, or with a reference for which an application for registration has already been submitted earlier pursuant to this article and confusion is to be feared as a result;
c. is misleading for voters in another sense;
d. is counter to public order.

A political party may apply to the Electoral Council in writing for an amendment of a registered reference.

The Electoral Council will cancel the registration of a political party if:

a. the party has submitted a request for this;
b. the party has ceased to exist;
c. the Articles of Association of the party have been amended in such a manner that they no longer comply with the requirements of this national ordinance;
d. the association is dissolved.

The Electoral Council shall resolve to scrap the registered reference of a political party:

a. in the cases mentioned above;
b. if the party failed to submit a list of candidates for the last parliamentary election.

On the amendment of its Articles of Association, a registered political party shall send the Electoral Council a copy of the notarized deed in which the amendment is laid down.

The Decisions of the Electoral Council

The decision of the Electoral Council on an application from a political party for registration and regarding an application to register a reference of a political party or to alter a reference shall be issued to the applicant and the

Central Voting Bureau in writing without delay and shall be published as soon as possible in the publication in which the country publishes official notices (*National Gazette*), as well as in one or more national daily newspapers.

For the articles of association of a political party, as well as amendments to these, they shall be published at the party's expense in the *National Gazette*.

Finally, an interested party may file an appeal against a decision pursuant to these decisions of the Electoral Council with the Court of First Instance.

The appeal must be submitted no later than the sixth day following the date of the publication in which the country publishes official notices and in which the decision is included.

Please note that no appeal is open against the decision of the Court of First Instance.

The Financial Administration of Political Parties

The board of a registered political party shall keep financial accounts such that all rights and obligations and the payments and receipts can be ascertained at all times. The accounts and the accompanying documents shall be kept for at least five years.

Each year before April 1, the registered political party shall send the Electoral Council an annual report including at least the following information:

a. the composition of the management during that year;
b. the number of contributing members at the start and end of that year;
c. the amount of the contribution during that year;
d. the activities performed by the party during that year.

The annual report shall be accompanied by financial statements, at least including:

a. the financial position at the start and end of the year;
b. a specified statement of income and expenditure, as well as an auditor's report by a chartered accountant concerning whether the financial statements present a true and fair view;
c. donations of ANG 5,000 or more from a source other than a natural person;
d. the total donations, other than contributions from party members.

On the disclosure of donations from a source other than a natural person as referred to, the amount and the date on which the donation was made, and the name of the donor shall be reported.

If the donor has objected to the disclosure of its name, this may be omitted, on the understanding that in that case, a reference shall be provided of the category of institutions to which the donor belongs.

The Electoral Council shall send the financial report to the General Audit Chamber in order to verify the accuracy of the information in the aforementioned report.

The General Audit Chamber shall send its advisory report to the Electoral Council.

The Electoral Council shall ensure that the annual report and the financial statements are available for public inspection.

The Electoral Council may impose further rules regarding the financial accounts, the annual report, and the financial statements.

Before taking effect, these rules require approval by national decree.

Donations to Registered Political Parties and Candidates

For the purpose of the application of this section, 'donations' refers to all sums of money received by a registered political party or a candidate and goods and services provided that are valuable in money, for which no consideration, or no equivalent financial consideration or consideration valuable in money is paid.

With a nonequivalent consideration, the amount of the donation is deemed to be the difference between the usual market price and the price actually paid.

A political party shall maintain permanent chronological records of all donations received.

Candidates for membership of Parliament shall maintain records of all donations that they receive from the date of their appointment by the party management to the date of the election.

The record of each donation shall state:

a. the name and address of the person, company, or institution that made the donation;
b. the amount or value of the donation;
c. the date of the donation.

A political party or a candidate shall accept donations of a sum or a value in excess of ANG 5,000 only if these originate from:

a. residents of St. Maarten with the right to vote;
b. non-Dutch residents of St. Maarten who were residents for at least five years prior to the date on which the donation was made;
c. legal persons (businesses) and social organizations registered in St. Maarten.

A political party and a candidate shall not accept donations from legal persons in which the country participates (for example government-owned companies) or from institutions subsidized by the government (for example foundations subsidized by government).

Important to note is that donations made to a natural person, legal person, or organization with the intention that such donations shall benefit a political party or candidate are regarded as donations to the relevant party or candidate.

In any calendar year, donations as referred to in article 32, made to the same political party by a person, company, or institution shall not exceed a total sum or value of ANG 30,000.

In any calendar year, donations as referred to in article 32, made to a candidate of a political party by a person, company, or institution shall not exceed a total sum or value of ANG 20,000.

In any calendar year, donations made to the same political party and to candidates of that same political party by a person, company, or institution shall not exceed a total sum of ANG 50,000.

Donations in excess of the maximum set mentioned above, shall not be accepted or shall be returned to the donor.

Cash donations to a political party or a candidate in excess of ANG 5,000 are prohibited. These donations shall not be accepted by a political party or candidate and shall be returned to the donor.

The Obligation to Report Donations

Each year before February 1, a party shall submit to the Electoral Council a copy of the section of the records kept by the party concerning the preceding year, accompanied by a declaration signed by the party.

Within a month following the date of the parliamentary elections, a candidate shall submit to the Electoral Council a copy of the records of donations kept by the candidate, accompanied by a declaration signed by the candidate.

At the request of the Electoral Council, the General Audit Chamber shall examine the accuracy of the statements made. The General Audit Chamber shall record the outcome of its examination in a report.

The political parties and the candidates shall provide all information required for the examination and shall provide access to their financial accounts.

The Electoral Council shall make an anonym summary of the report available for public inspection.

Political parties and candidates shall keep the records of donations for at least five years. Copies of sections of records transferred to the Electoral Council shall be destroyed at the end of five years.

Supervision and Enforcement

As is mentioned, the Electoral Council is responsible for supervision of compliance with the rules laid down by or pursuant to the National Ordinance on the registration and finances of political parties.

The Electoral Council is therefore authorized, to the extent that this can reasonably be deemed to be necessary for the performance of its duties:

a. To request all information
b. To require access to all books, documents, and other data carriers and to take copies of these or to temporarily remove them for that purpose

All persons shall provide the assistance required by the Electoral Council.

The Electoral Council may impose an order subject to penalty regarding infringements of a regulation imposed by articles 26, 27, 28, 33, 34, 35, 37, 38(2), 40, 41, 42, and 43.

An order subject to penalty serves to reverse the infringement or to prevent further infringement or a repetition of the infringement.

The Electoral Council shall fix the penalty either as a lump sum or as an amount per unit of time in which the order is not implemented or per infringement of the order.

The council shall also fix an amount in excess of which no further penalty is due. The fixed amount shall be in reasonable proportion to the seriousness of the interest breached and the envisaged effect of the imposition of the penalty.

The following shall in any event be stated in the decision to impose an order subject to penalty:

  a. the name of the offender, and
  b. the content of the order and the term for which it applies.

In the decision to impose an order subject to penalty serving to reverse an infringement or to prevent further infringement, a term will be fixed during which the offender can carry out the order without a penalty being due.

On request, the Electoral Council shall give the offender an opportunity to view the information on which the intention to impose an order subject to penalty is based, and to make copies of this.

The Electoral Council shall give the offender an opportunity to present his or her views and the offender may submit an appeal against the imposition of the order.

The power to collect forfeited amounts lapses six months after the date on which they are forfeited.

The prescription period is suspended through bankruptcy or compulsory winding up and every statutory impediment to collection of the penalty.

At the request of the offender, the Electoral Council may cancel an order subject to penalty that it has imposed, suspend it for a particular term or reduce the penalty in the event of the permanent or temporary inability of the offender to meet its obligations, partially or in full.

At the request of the offender, the Electoral Council may cancel an order subject to penalty that it has imposed if the decision has been in effect for one year without the penalty being forfeited.

In the absence of compliance with the order within the term, the Electoral Council may provide for collection of the penalty plus the costs relating to collection by a writ of execution, unless an appeal has been submitted against the imposition of the order pursuant to the National Ordinance administrative jurisdiction.

A writ of execution as referred to in paragraph 1 shall be served by bailiff's writ at the expense of the offender and gives rise to entitlement to enforcement within the meaning of the Code of Civil Procedure.

For six weeks following the date of service, an appeal against the writ of execution may be filed by a summons of the Electoral Council. The appeal suspends the execution.

At the request of the Electoral Council, the court may cancel the suspension of the execution.

Forfeited penalties shall be deposited in the national treasury.

Obligations of Members of Parliament and Ministers

In accordance with article 53, a candidate who has been elected as a member of Parliament must submit to Parliament, together with his or her credentials, a declaration signed by the member that he or she did not act in contravention of the provisions of the National Ordinance on the registration and finances of political parties, during the election campaign.

The candidate, appointed as minister, must submit to the Electoral Council, within thirty days of accepting an appointment as minister, a declaration signed by him or her that the person did not act in contravention of the provisions of this national ordinance during the election campaign.

Actions in contravention of articles 26, 33, 34, 35, 40, 41, 42, and 53 shall be penalized by detention of no more than three months or a financial penalty of no more than ANG 10,000, or by both penalties.

With a conviction for the violations referred to, withdrawal of the rights referred to in article 32(1.1) of the Criminal Code may be ordered.

Confidentiality Obligation

Every person involved in the implementation of this national ordinance who gains access in that regard to information that he or she knows to be, or should reasonably assume to be, of a confidential nature and for whom a confidentiality obligation does not already apply on the grounds of the person's office, profession, or pursuant to statutory provisions, is required to protect the confidentiality of that information.

This does not apply:

a. in relation to the offences described in articles 198 and 200 of the Criminal Code;
b. to the extent that any statutory provision requires him or her to disclose information or the need to disclose information arises from his or her duties.

Prosecution for a breach of confidentiality shall be instituted only in response to a complaint by the person regarding whom confidentiality is breached.

Article 12 of the Election Ordinance
The Central Electoral Committee

In accordance with article 12 of the Election Ordinance, there shall be a Central Electoral Committee. This committee is also called the Central Voting Bureau and operates independently of Parliament and of the government.

The Central Voting Bureau consists of five members, including a chairman and a substitute chairman. There are also two substitute members.

The members are appointed by national decree based on their expertise and experience, on the nomination of the Appointment Committee. They are appointed for a term of seven years and may be reappointed on one occasion.

The main task of the Central Voting Bureau is to supervise the work of the Electoral Committees at the polling stations.

Next to that, throughout the Election Ordinance, the responsibility and tasks of the Central Voting Bureau is regulated. In discussing the procedures in organizing the elections, the role of the Central Voting Bureau will be mentioned.

CHAPTER 3

Election Rights and the Election Ordinance

Election Rights

One of the fundamental rights of the citizens of St. Maarten, regulated in the Constitution, is the right to vote, or as mentioned in article 23, election rights.

This article reads as follows:

> Every Dutch national residing in Sint Maarten shall have equal rights to elect the members of general representative bodies and (has the right) to stand for election as a member of those bodies, subject to exceptions laid down by national ordinance.

The rights mentioned in this article are called active and passive voting rights. The active right is to elect the members of general representative bodies, and the passive right is to stand for election as a member of those bodies. As mentioned, these rights are given a place in the Constitution of St. Maarten as an independent fundamental right.

The term *equal* reflects the principle of "one man, one vote." Consequently, it is not permissible to assign multiple voting rights to certain qualified persons.

The representative body referred to in the article is the Parliament of St. Maarten.

It should also be clear that in a community regulated by laws, the possibility of restrictions of the fundamental right to active and passive election rights is essential. An age limit, for example, must inevitably be imposed. Other examples of restrictions are residency and Dutch nationality.

Reference should also be made to the withdrawal of election rights by the courts as an additional penalty and the temporary exclusion from the right to stand for election of holders of political authority who have been finally convicted according to the provisions of articles 36 and 50 of the Constitution.

Please note, however, that as mentioned in article 23, any restriction to this fundamental right should be done by national ordinance. By doing this, Parliament, the representative of the people of Sint Maarten, is involved and has the last word.

According to article 55 paragraph one of the Constitution, further rules will be laid down by national ordinance in relation to the right to vote and to the elections.

This was done among others, by establishing the Election Ordinance, issued on December 20, 2010, by the minister of general affairs, (A.B.2010, GT no. 10).

When drafting this election ordinance, the following main points were taken into consideration:

1. The main elements of the right to vote, such as the nomination of candidates, the election system, in comparison with the right to vote for Parliament in both the Netherlands Antilles and Aruba, remained the same, and also the system of lists and not persons.
2. The distribution of seats, as regulated in the Island Ordinance of St. Maarten of 1999—namely, that if fewer candidates on a list than the number of seats assigned to that list have won a number of votes equal to or in excess of the list quota, the candidates

are ordered according to the number of votes that they have won, starting with the candidate who won the highest number of votes.

The Election Ordinance

The will of the people is expressed in direct, regular, free, and confidential parliamentary elections. This principle, as well as the right to vote as laid down in article 24 of the Constitution and a number of provisions in chapter 4 of the Constitution concerning the election of members of Parliament, forms the basis for the Election Ordinance.

Based on article 2 of the Election Ordinance, members of Parliament are elected directly by persons who, on the thirtieth day prior to that of the submission of nominations referred to in article 21 of the same ordinance, are residents of Sint Maarten, hold Dutch nationality, and on the date of the election, have reached the age of eighteen.

The age limit and the requirement of residency and Dutch nationality for exercising the right to vote are consistent with article 46 of the Charter for the Kingdom and articles 23 and 48 of the Constitution. These requirements are also consistent with the code of good practice in electoral matters of the European Commission for Democracy through Law (Venice Commission).

Chapter 3 of the Election Ordinance Refers to the Electoral Register.

This is a register hold by the Department of Civil Registry (under the responsibility of the minister of general affairs). More specifically, in accordance with article 4 of the election ordinance, this register is to identify who is a resident and is entitled to vote.

As is mentioned in article 4, an electoral register shall be maintained, listing the persons recorded in the basic administration of personal records (who are entitled to vote).

For each voter, the surname, first names, the place and date of birth, the address, and the number of the polling district to which the voter belongs shall be recorded in the electoral register. Married women and widows shall be recorded in the electoral register under the name of their husbands or late husbands, adding their maiden name preceded by the term "born" or an abbreviation of that term, in accordance with article 6.

Furthermore, based on article 8, the minister of general affairs is required, free of charge and on request, to provide all members of the public with the information in the electoral register from which they can determine whether they or another person, provided that they are authorized for that purpose, are correctly recorded in the register.

All persons have the right at all times to petition the court of first instance for an addition to or improvement of the electoral register, on the grounds that they, or another person, provided that they are authorized for that purpose, have or have not been included in the register, or have not been included correctly, in contravention of the provisions of this national ordinance.

A form that is available free of charge at the Department of the Civil Registry shall be used for the purpose of the petition. The procedures are elaborated in article 9 and further of the Election Ordinance.

Organizing the Elections

When a date is established for elections, a few steps need to be taken in organizing the elections.

It is mentioned in article 21 of the Election Ordinance that the date shall be enacted by national decree on the proposal of the minister of general affairs, on a date between the ninetieth and eightieth day before the end of the parliamentary term, or before the date on which Parliament will be dissolved.[4]

Based on article 22, on the mentioned date, political parties registered with the Electoral Council referred to in article 3 of the National Ordinance registration and finances of political parties[5] may submit lists of candidates to the chairman of the Central Voting Bureau or to a member of that committee to be designated by the chairman, at the location where the committee is established, between 9:00 a.m. and 4:00 p.m. Forms that are available from the Census Office free of charge shall be used for these lists. The form and design of the list of candidates shall be enacted by national decree, containing general measures.

Three weeks prior to the date for the nomination of candidates, the information mentioned above shall be published by or on behalf of the chairman of the Central Voting Bureau.

---

[4] Please note that the national decree is on the proposal of the minister. This means that the minister will propose the content to the governor, and when the governor is in agreement, by signing the draft national decree, the minister will then cosign the national decree and make sure that it is published.

[5] AB 2010, GT no. 11

Nomination and Support

In accordance with article 23, each list of candidates must be supported by a number of voters equal to 1 percent of the voting figures recorded by the Central Voting Bureau at the last election held, rounded up to a whole number.

The support shall be shown by the placement of signatures on each list of candidates by the voters at the Census Office during the day following that of the submission of the lists (postulation day), from 9:00 a.m. to 4:00 p.m.

The voter may sign only one list or copy thereof.
To be allowed to sign one of the lists, the voter should provide proof of identity through:

a. a valid identity card within the meaning of article 1 of the National Ordinance identity cards (P.B. 1965, No. 17);
b. a valid passport;
c. a valid driver's license;
d. any valid proof of identity to be designated by another national decree, containing general measures.

Please note that the support mentioned does not apply regarding a list of candidates of a political party to which one or more seats in Parliament were assigned at the last election held.

The List for Nomination and the Candidates

Article 24 regulates how the names of the candidates should be mentioned on the list.

The following is important to note:

a. If a candidate is a married woman or widow, she shall be included in the list with the name of her husband or late husband, adding her maiden name, preceded by the term "born" or an abbreviation thereof, or with her maiden name only.
b. The number of candidates permissible is also mentioned—namely that a list of candidates may contain at most eight more candidates than the number of members to be elected. In the case of the Parliament of St. Maarten, this number is still fifteen, therefore a list may contain a maximum of twenty-three candidates.
c. The description of the party, as registered with the Electoral Council, is placed at the top of the list.

Furthermore, in accordance with article 25, every candidate on the list needs to hand in a written declaration declaring his or her consent to nomination on that list, together with the list.

A form available free of charge from the Department of Civil Registry shall be used for that declaration. The form and the format of that declaration shall be enacted by national decree, containing general measures.

If the candidate is located outside Sint Maarten, the declaration is not bound by any form and may also be made by means other than by handing in.

Please note that this declaration of consent once handed in cannot be withdrawn.

Next to the mentioned declaration of the candidates, when handing in the list, the following shall also be submitted:

a. a declaration by or on behalf of the chairman of the Central Voting Bureau that the candidate has the right to stand for election;

b. a written declaration (receipt), that ANG 2,000 was deposited, in the name of one of the persons recorded in the electoral register;

c. a black and white photograph measuring four by six centimeters, presenting a clear and faithful image of the highest-placed candidate.

It is important to mention that the amount referred to under b. shall be returned to the entitled person, after the election results are known, unless:

a. the list for which the amount was deposited is declared invalid;

b. or, the voting figure for the list for which the amount is deposited is less than the electoral quota.

Once the decision is made that the amount is not refunded to the person in whose name it was deposited, it reverts to the national treasury.

On the third day, after the procedure for the support of the list has been finalized, the Central Voting Bureau will conduct a session to examine the candidate lists.

The following omissions can be detected:

a. that the list is not supported by the required number of authorized voters. In the assessment of whether a list meets this requirement, the signatories who have signed more than one list or copy of a list shall be disregarded;

b. that the surname, first names, initials, date of birth, domicile, or address of a candidate are not recorded;

   c. that a married woman or widow on the list is not recorded in accordance with the provisions of article 24, paragraph 2;

   d. that a candidate's declaration that he or she consents to the nomination on the list has not been provided;

   e. that in the opinion of the Central Voting Bureau, the photograph provided does not comply with the requirements as mentioned in the law;[6]

   f. that no description of the political party has been placed above the list, or the description differs from the registered description.

Based on the above, the Central Voting Bureau will notify the persons who submitted the list, by registered mail or for a signed receipt, no later than the following day.

Within three days of the date on which the mentioned notification is issued, the person who submitted the list may correct the omission(s) described in the notice before the Central Voting Bureau. If the person who submitted the list is absent or indisposed, one of the candidates on

---

[6] in observance of paragraphs 3 and 4 of this article, the Central Voting Bureau shall grant the person who submitted the photograph an opportunity to submit a new photograph; if, in the opinion of the Central Electoral Committee, the new photograph also fails to comply with the requirements set, the Central Electoral Committee shall decide at its session as referred to in article 36(1), that the list in question will be printed on the ballot paper referred to in article 56(1) without a photograph.

the list shall deputize for him or her, in the order in which they appear on the list.

No later than the third day mentioned above, after the omissions have to be corrected, the Central Voting Bureau will decide at a public session on the validity of the lists, on the maintenance of the candidates included in those lists, and on the maintenance of the description of a political party at the top of each list.

The date and time of the session will be publicized by or on behalf of the chairman.

A list is invalid when:

a. it is not submitted to the chairman of the Central Voting Bureau or to the member designated by the chairman on the nomination date between 9:00 a.m. and 4:00 p.m.;
b. it is not supported by the required number of authorized voters;
c. it does not comply with the provisions regarding form and design regulated by national decree, containing general measures;
d. it is not submitted personally by one of the persons referred to in the law;
e. all candidates on it have been scrapped;

    f. the declaration prescribed has not been added;

    g. no description is placed on it or a description that differs from the description registered with the Electoral Council.

Within two days of the date on which the Central Voting Bureau decides on the validity of the lists, and if the candidates and the descriptions of the political party as mentioned on the top of the list will be maintained, any voter may appeal that decision before the Court of First Instance.

According to article 34, the court shall hear the appeal in a public session to be held within fourteen days of the date on which the appeal is received. During the hearing, the appellant may explain the appeal, and the chairman, or another member of the Central Voting Bureau, may explain the decision of the committee in further detail.

The court shall decide on the appeal no later than on the third day following the mentioned session. The clerk of the court shall notify the appellant, the person who submitted the list, and the Central Voting Bureau of the decision without delay.

It is important to note that no further appeal may be filed against the decision of the court.

However, please also note that if an appeal is filed against a decision of the Central Voting Bureau declaring a list to be invalid or having deleted a candidate on the mentioned grounds without issuing notice to the person who submitted the list of the existence of that omission in advance, the omission may still be corrected by that person. This can be done by the clerk of the Court of First Instance, where the appeal is filed.

Numbers and Colors of Political Parties

As soon as the term of two days for appeal referred to in article 33 has expired or, in the event of an appeal, the Central Voting Bureau has been notified of the decision of the court, the Central Voting Bureau shall number the lists in the sequence designated by lot in a session open to voters, as prescribed by article 36.

During that session, the persons who submitted lists, or one of the candidates who deputizes for that person, may notify the chairman of the Central Voting Bureau in writing of their preferred color for that list. A receipt will be handed over by or on behalf of the chairman of the Central Voting Bureau to the person who submitted the notice. The only colors that may be chosen are those announced for each election by national decree of the minister of general affairs, at least fourteen days prior to the date of the nominations. As soon as possible, the chairman of the Central Voting Bureau will send a copy of this national decree to the persons who submitted the lists of candidates.

The following rules will apply in assigning the colors.

1. The list(s) for which a color preference has been notified will be assigned that color.
2. If the same color is selected in two or more notices, that color will be assigned to the list to which that color was assigned in the last election held;
3. or, if this was not the case, the decision shall be made by lot.
4. Colors will be assigned by lot to the other list(s) concerned and to the list(s) for which no notice of color preference was submitted.
5. The lots will be drawn at the session of the Central Voting Bureau.

The date and time of the session of the Central Voting Bureau and the possibility of submitting mentioned notice shall be published in advance.

In accordance with article 37, the Central Voting Bureau shall publish the lists at the earliest opportunity. The publication shall take place by making the lists of candidates available for public inspection at the Civil Registry, while at the same time, the chairman of the Central Voting Bureau shall make public that the lists are available for public inspection.

Voting

The date of voting for the election of members of Parliament shall be enacted by national decree on the proposal of the minister of general affairs, in such a manner that at least forty-eight days lie between the date of the nominations and that of voting.

Voting shall commence at 8:00 a.m. and shall continue until 8:00 p.m.

Every employer is required to ensure that every voter in its employ has an opportunity to vote, to the extent that this cannot take place within the established working hours and provided that the voter is not prevented from performing his or her work by this for more than two hours.

The board and management of an institution for medical treatment, nursing, or care shall give persons admitted to that institution who are entitled to vote an opportunity to do so if there are no objections on medical grounds to voting by the person concerned.

At least three days prior to the date of the vote, the minister of general affairs shall announce the date and times at which voting will take place and the contents of articles 131, 132, 133, 134, and 135 of the Criminal Code of Sint Maarten.

Voting shall take place only at the polling station of the polling district to which the voter is assigned.

For the voting, Sint Maarten shall be divided into polling districts by national decree, containing general measures. As a rule, a polling district shall not contain more than fifteen hundred voters.

As regulated by article 39, voting shall take place only on the lists declared valid and the candidates appearing in these lists.

Only persons who are recorded in the electoral register on the thirtieth day prior to the date of the nominations are eligible to vote, as referred to in article 21.

In accordance with article 43, at least eight days prior to the voting date, every voter eligible to vote shall receive a polling card from the head of the Civil Registry calling on them to vote.

This card shall state:

a. that a parliamentary election shall take place;

b. the surname, first names, date and place of birth, and address of the voter;

c. the number under which the voter appears in the copy of or extract from the electoral register to be used in the vote;

d. the number of the polling district to which the voter is assigned;

e. the address of the polling station for that polling district;

f. the date and times at which voting will take place.

The form, design, and color of the polling card shall be enacted by national decree, containing general measures.

Voters shall be notified of the lists of candidates, by showing these lists:

- on the polling cards or by sending these to the address of the voters in printed form, at the same time as the polling card;
- or otherwise, at least eight days prior to the date of the vote,
- or by displaying these in printed form at the entrance to the polling station on the day of the vote.

These lists of candidates shall state the surnames and first names or initials of the candidates, as well as the descriptions of the political parties and the list numbers. With the name of each candidate, the number showing his or her rank on the list shall also be shown on the list concerned.

Voters entitled to vote who have been sent a polling card but whose polling card has been lost or was not received, shall be issued with a new polling card by the Department of the Civil Registry, on request, if they can provide adequate proof of identity.

Please note that at the polling districts, the Electoral Committees are also authorized to issue such cards.

The Electoral Committees

There shall be an Electoral Committee for each polling district.

Each Electoral Committee shall consist of three members, including a chairman. The chairman is the first member of the Electoral Committee, and one of the two members shall be appointed as the second member and one as the third member of the Electoral Committee. Furthermore, at least two deputy members shall be appointed for the committee.

The chairman, members, and deputy members of the Electoral Committees shall be appointed by the minister of general affairs from among residents entitled to vote. The appointment shall take place in good time before the voting date, with simultaneous resignation of the serving chairman, members, and deputy members. The minister of general affairs shall designate suitable accommodation for each polling district. The financial provisions for the members and deputy members of the Electoral Committee shall be regulated by national decree, containing general measures.

The chairman, members, or deputy members of the Electoral Committee, which are present on the opening of the session of the Electoral Committee, shall take part in voting at this polling district. If, according to the electoral register, they are assigned to a different polling district, the casting of their votes will be included in the procès-verbal of the session.

At all times during the session, the chairman and at least two members of the Electoral Committee must be present. If the chairman is absent, those members shall deputize for him or her, by order of appointment.

If a member is absent, a deputy member designated by the chairman shall deputize for him or her. In the case that no deputy member is available, the chairman shall request voters present in the polling station whom he or she regards as suitable for that purpose, to serve as such for the time being, until a deputy member is available.

In the performance of their duties, members of the Electoral Committee shall not reveal their political views in any way. If votes are tied regarding a decision by the Electoral Committee, the chairman has the casting vote.

Finally, any changes made in the membership of the Electoral Committee should be noted in the official process-verbal. This notification should include the reasons for this and the date of the replacement.

The Polling Station, Polling Booth, and the Ballot Box

The head of the Department of Civil Registry shall provide for the layout of the polling station, in such a manner that the confidentiality of votes is assured.

The polling station shall contain a table for the Electoral Committee, a ballot box, and one or more entirely separate polling booths or one or more voting machines. Access to the polling booths must be visible to the public.

Each polling booth will contain a guide for the voter. A model for the guide shall be enacted by ministerial regulation. The table for the Electoral Committee shall be positioned so that voters can observe the actions of the Electoral Committee.

A copy of the data from the electoral register, containing a numbered list of the voters authorized to vote in the polling district, shall be placed on the table for the Electoral Committee. The data contained in this list shall be enacted by national decree, containing general measures.

Each Electoral Committee shall have a copy of the relevant laws, regulations, and procedures relating to voting.

The ballot box shall stand next to the table, within reach of the member of the Electoral Committee who ensures that the voter places the ballot paper in the ballot box.

The Electoral Committee shall close the ballot box in good time before the start, having assured itself that the box is empty.

Further rules concerning the layout of polling stations may be enacted by national decree, containing general measures.

This is also the case for the ballot boxes, which should be produced in accordance with regulations to be enacted by national decree, containing general measures.

The Ballot Papers

The description of the political party and the lists of the candidates for which votes can be cast, as notified to the voters, shall be printed on one side of the ballot paper to be used for the election and the signature of the chairman of the Central Voting Bureau on the other. The side on which the signature of the chairman of the Central Voting Bureau is printed may state that this concerns elections for the Parliament of Sint Maarten and a specification of the constituency.

A model for the ballot paper shall be enacted by ministerial regulation.

The head of the Department of Civil Registry shall determine the number of ballot papers required, taking account of the fact that ballot papers must be available for each Electoral Committee for the number of voters authorized to vote in the polling district plus at least an extra two per hundred.

The head of mentioned department shall ensure that the necessary ballot papers are available to each Electoral Committee before voting commences.

The ballot papers shall be sent to the Electoral Committee in one or more sealed packages, each showing the number of the polling district and the number of ballot papers that it contains. The Electoral Committee shall open the packages containing ballot papers in good time before voting commences and shall determine the number of ballot papers.

Voting Machines

Voting machines may be used instead of ballot papers. In that case, the provisions of this national ordinance that concern the use of ballot papers shall not apply.

Voting machines are currently not being used in Sint Maarten.
In case Sint Maarten chooses to use voting machines, there will be no need to adjust and regulate such, since the use is regulated in articles 59 to 64 of the Election Ordinance and in some other articles.

The Voter

Only persons authorized to vote in the elections shall be permitted to vote, providing that they possess the prescribed polling card and can show proof of identity by means of evidence as mentioned in the national ordinance.

The voter shall hand the polling card to the chairman of the Electoral Committee. The chairman shall clearly state the number under which the voter appears in the copy of or extract from the electoral register, according to the polling card.

The second member of the Electoral Committee shall state the name shown in the copy of or extract from the electoral register for the number stated by the chairman. The chairman shall check the name against the polling card.

The second member of the Electoral Committee shall record that the voter has reported for voting by placing his or her initials next to the voter's name in the copy of or extract from the electoral register.

The chairman shall then hand the voter a ballot paper, folded so that the signature of the chairman of the Central Voting Bureau is visible. The chairman shall keep a record of the number of ballot papers issued and of the number of voters that refuse to take receipt of a ballot paper.

Following receipt of the ballot paper, the voter goes to a polling booth that is not in use and votes by using a red pencil to mark a white box in the voting column alongside the name of the candidate of his or her choice.

The voter then folds the ballot paper in such a way that the names of the candidates are not visible and immediately takes this to the ballot box.

The third member of the Electoral Committee, without taking hold of the ballot paper, assures himself or herself that it contains the signature of the chairman of the Central Voting Bureau and instructs the voter to place the ballot paper in the ballot box. That person keeps a record of the number of ballot papers placed in the ballot box.

If the voter makes a mistake in completing the ballot paper, he or she returns this to the chairman. The chairman will issue the voter with a new ballot paper on request, on one occasion only. The chairman immediately makes returned ballot papers unusable by stamping the word "unusable" on both sides of the ballot paper.

If the Electoral Committee observes that a voter requires assistance due to his or her physical condition, the voter may be provided support.

A voter who fails to comply with the regulations concerning voting, following a warning, will not be admitted to the ballot box and is required to return the ballot paper if this has already been handed to him or her.

A voter admitted to the polling booth who refuses to place the ballot paper in the ballot box is required to return the ballot paper.

Also, the chairman immediately makes returned ballot papers unusable by stamping the word "unusable" on both sides of the ballot paper.

If a voter refuses to return the ballot paper, the chairman shall make a note of this, recording the name and the number shown on the polling card.

While the Electoral Committee is in session, voters are authorized to stay in the polling station, to the extent that this does not disturb public order or obstruct the progress of the session.

The voters present in the polling station may submit objections orally, if voting does not take place in accordance with the regulations. The objections will be reported in the procès-verbal of the session of the Electoral Committee.

No activities that are intended to influence the choice of the voters shall take place in the polling station.

The chairman is responsible for maintaining public order in the polling station during the session. He or she may request support from the minister of justice.

If, in the view of the Electoral Committee, circumstances arise in or near the polling station that make the proper progress of the session impossible, the chairman shall declare this. The session is thereupon suspended.

The chairman shall notify the minister of general affairs of this without delay, who will then determine when and where the session will be resumed.

Further rules regarding this shall be imposed by or pursuant to an order, containing general measures.

The End of the Voting

As soon as the time set for voting has expired, this will be announced by the chairman, and only the voters who are present in or at the door of the polling station at the time of that announcement will still be admitted to vote.

After the last of the voters has voted, the opening of the ballot box will be closed and sealed.

Immediately after voting has ended, the Electoral Committee shall determine:

a. the number of voters who reported for voting;
b. the number of ballot papers issued;
c. the number of ballot papers placed in the ballot box;

    d. the number of voters who refused to take receipt of a ballot paper;

    e. the number of ballot papers returned and made unusable;

    f. the number of unused ballot papers.

The chairman shall announce the numbers referred to to the voters present.

The Electoral Committee shall then report and certify the number of initials placed on the copy of, or extract from, the electoral register. This copy or extract shall be placed in a package to be sealed separately.

Finally, the following shall be packaged in the same manner:

    a. the unused ballot papers;

    b. the returned ballot papers made unusable;

    c. the polling cards handed in.

Immediately after the sealing of mentioned documents, the ballot box shall be opened. However, the Electoral Committee may leave a space of no more than one hour between the sealing and the opening of the ballot box, provided that they don't leave the polling station and the ballot box is kept under supervision. In a situation like this, it will be noted in the procès-verbal of the vote, as will the compliance with the conditions set for this.

Counting the Ballot Papers

The ballot papers shall be mixed and counted, and their number shall be compared with the number of voters who took part in the vote.

The members of the Electoral Committee shall open the ballot papers and combine these by list. They may use the support of deputy members for this work. The chairman then reports the name of the candidate for whom a vote has been cast, by list, for each ballot paper. Both the other members keep notes of each vote cast, after the oldest of them has examined the ballot paper.

Regarding each list, the Electoral Committee determines:

    a. the number of votes cast for each candidate;
    b. the total number of votes, as referred to in paragraph a.

Invalid Ballots

Ballot papers other than those that may be used by or pursuant to the provisions of this national ordinance are invalid.

The following ballot papers are also invalid:

a. those in which no white box has been colored red in any voting column;

b. those in which a white box has been colored red in more than one voting column;

c. those in which the voter has cast a vote by means other than with red pencil;

d. those in which additions have been made or which contain an indication of the voter;

e. those that do not contain the prescribed signature.

Please note that a white box that has been partially colored red in the voting column next to the name of a candidate is deemed to have been fully colored red if this appears to be consistent with the intention of the voter.

The Electoral Committee decides on the validity of the ballot paper, taking the above into consideration. The chairman immediately announces the reason for a declaration of invalidity and for doubts regarding validity, as well as the decision in that regard. Both the other members keep notes of each ballot paper declared valid.

If one of the voters present so requires, the paper must be shown. The voters may submit objections orally to the decision taken.

Announcements by the Chair

As soon as the votes have been recorded, the chairman announces:

a. for each list the number of votes cast for each candidate as well as the total number of votes cast.

The voters present may submit objections.

The ballot papers declared invalid are then placed in a sealable package showing the number of the polling district and the number of ballot papers that the package contains.

The valid ballot papers are then sealed in one or more packages, ordered by list. Each package shows the number of the polling district and the number of ballot papers that the package contains, as well as the numbers of the lists to which the enclosed papers relate if the papers are sealed in more than one package.

The chairman then announces:

b. the number of votes cast for each candidate, by list.

For each list, the Electoral Committee determines the total number of votes cast for candidates appearing on that list.

c. The chairman announces this.

The voters present may submit objections.

The chairman than locks the area in which the counters are located. The key is placed in a sealed envelope.

On completion, an official procès-verbal is immediately drawn up of the voting and the counting of the votes, in duplicate. All objections submitted are recorded in the procès-verbal. The procès-verbal is signed by all members of the Electoral Committee.[7]

The chairman or a member of the Electoral Committee designated by the chairman shall take the procès-verbal and the sealed packages to the chairman of the Central Voting Bureau.

---

[7] A model for the procès-verbal shall be enacted by ministerial regulation.

Determination of the Election Results and the Voting Figure by the Central Voting Bureau

At 10:00 a.m. on the fifth day following the vote, the Central Voting Bureau shall conduct a public session. Voters are authorized to stay in the location intended for the public, to the extent that this does not disturb public order or obstruct the progress of the work. The chairman is responsible for maintaining public order during the session and may request assistance for this from the minister of justice.

In this session, the Central Voting Bureau may order a new count of ballot papers from all or from one or more polling districts, either officially or in response to a request from one or more voters, stating the reasons.

In that case, the Central Voting Bureau shall immediately start that recount.

The Central Voting Bureau is authorized to open the sealed packages for that purpose and to compare the contents with the procès-verbal of the Electoral Committees.

The Central Voting Bureau shall determine regarding each list the number of votes cast for each candidate and the total of these votes. This total is referred to as "the voting figure."

The chairman announces the results obtained, and the voters present may submit objections orally.

A procès-verbal of this shall be drawn up immediately, including all objections raised. The official procès-verbal shall be signed by all members of the Central Voting Bureau in attendance.[8]

The chairman shall immediately make the procès-verbal of the session of the Central Voting Bureau available for public inspection at the Department of Civil Registry.

After the Central Voting Bureau has determined the result of the election and decisions have been made on the admission of the elected representatives, the chairman shall destroy the sealed packages.

At the end of the period in which the election took place, the chairman shall destroy the procès-verbal of the Electoral Committees if desired. An official procès-verbal shall be drawn up of the destruction.

The prescribed sealing shall take place with the coat of arms of Sint Maarten as the seal.

---

[8] A model for the procès-verbal shall be enacted by ministerial regulation.

CHAPTER 4

Following the Elections

The Elected Members of Parliament

After the Central Voting Bureau has determined the result of the election and in taking the decisions on the admission of the elected representatives, the next steps are relevant.

In accordance with article 94 of the Election Ordinance, as soon as possible following the session to determine the outcome of the elections, the Central Voting Bureau shall determine the result of the election by an order.

The Electoral Quota, the List Quota, and the Elected members of Parliament

Based on article 95, the Central Voting Bureau shall divide the sum of the voting figures of all lists by the number of seats to be filled. The quotient obtained in this manner is referred to as the electoral quota.

Consequently, vacant seats will be assigned to a list as many times as the electoral quota is included in the voting figure of that list.

Following that exercise, the seats still to be filled will be assigned, in sequence, to the list that after the assignment of the seat will show the highest average number of votes per assigned seat. If the averages are the same, the decision shall be made by lot.

Please note that lists for which the voting figure[9] is less than the electoral quota shall be disregarded in this assignment.

The Central Voting Bureau shall divide the voting figure of the list by the number of seats assigned to the list. In accordance with article 97, this is called the list quota.

It should be mentioned that for the purpose of filling the seats assigned to each list, the candidates on the list that won a number of votes equal to or in excess of the list quota are elected. If fewer candidates on a list than the number of seats assigned to that list have won a number of

---

[9] Remember, the Central Electoral Committee shall determine regarding each list the number of votes cast for each candidate and the total of these votes. This total is referred to as "the voting figure."

votes equal to or in excess of the list quota, the candidates are ordered according to the number of votes that they have won, starting with the candidate who won the highest number of votes. The seats are assigned in order of the highest candidates on the list who have not yet been elected.

After this exercise, the Central Voting Bureau shall order the candidates included in each list in order of the number of votes that they won, starting with the candidate who won the highest number of votes. If candidates have won an equal number of votes, the order shall be determined by their order on the list.

The chairman of the Central Voting Bureau shall announce the election result at the earliest opportunity in a public session.

The order by which the election result is established shall be published through inclusion in the *National Gazette* of Sint Maarten and through provision for public inspection at the Census Office. This in accordance with article 102.

Notification to Parliament and the Elected Candidates

The chairman of the Central Voting Bureau shall provide for Parliament to be sent copies of the following documents:

   a. the official procès-verbal of the sessions of the Electoral Committees;

   b. the official procès-verbal of the session of the Central Voting Bureau;

   c. the official procès-verbal of the session of the Central Voting Bureau;

   d. the order of the Central Voting Bureau;

   e. the official procès-verbal of the session of the Central Voting Bureau.

The chairman of the Central Voting Bureau shall notify the elected representative of being elected, by a letter signed by the chairman. This letter should be sent in duplicate within three days of the determination of the election result or after the declaration that the candidate has been elected, by registered mail or for a signed receipt. The letter shall be sent to the address of the elected representative as shown with the nomination or if the elected representative has reported a different address later, to that address.

Within five days of the receipt of the notice, the elected representative shall issue a signed confirmation of receipt. Within two weeks of the signature of the notice of election, the chairman of the Central Voting Bureau must receive written notice from the elected representative that the elected representative accepts his or her election. If the notice is not received within that term, the elected representative is deemed to have rejected the election. The chairman shall notify Parliament of the rejection of the election.

Furthermore, the chairman shall notify the elected representative and Parliament without delay of the receipt of the notice of acceptance of the election, in duplicate.

The Credentials

Please note that this notice of the chairman of the Electoral Council to Parliament and the notification of the chairman to the elected representative of being elected serves as credentials.

Elected representatives must submit their credentials within three weeks of the signature of the notice of election, to Parliament. If the credentials are not submitted within the mentioned term, the seat is deemed to have fallen vacant on the first day following the date of the expiration of that term. When this happens, the president of Parliament shall notify the Central Voting Bureau of this, without delay.

Together with his or her credentials, the elected representative presents to Parliament a signed declaration reporting all public positions that the person holds. If the elected representative has not previously been admitted as a member of Parliament, he or she shall also submit an extract from the basic administration of personal records or, in the absence thereof, an identification certificate, showing his or her date and place of birth.

Parliament shall examine the credentials and shall decide whether the elected representative shall be admitted as a member of Parliament. In that process, Parliament checks whether the elected representative complies with the requirements for membership and does not hold any positions incompatible with membership and decides on any disputes that arise regarding the credentials or to the election itself.

Please note that the examination of the credentials does not extend to the validity of the lists, as published by the Central Voting Bureau.

Furthermore, the examination of the credentials of candidates who are declared to have been elected does not extend to the matters relating to the validity of the voting.

No Admittance by Parliament

In accordance with article 110, if Parliament decides not to admit one or more elected representatives due to the invalidity of the voting in one or more polling districts, the chairman shall notify the minister of general affairs of this, without delay. Within one month of the receipt of this notification, a new vote shall take place in the mentioned polling districts, and the result of the election shall be determined (again).

Please note that in this determination, candidates who have already been admitted as members of Parliament are still declared elected, even if this proves to have taken place incorrectly. The candidate who would have been elected if the admitted candidate had not been declared elected is then rejected.

If Parliament decides not to admit one or more elected candidates on the grounds of the inaccuracy of the determination of the election result, the chairman shall notify the Central Voting Bureau of this without delay.

Within eight days of the receipt of this notification, the Central Voting Bureau shall conduct a session open to voters and shall, if necessary, redetermine the result of the election in observance of the decision of the parliament.

Please note that the examination of the credentials of the new candidate declared to have been elected in this way does not extend to the points concerning the validity of the votes.

Furthermore, Parliament can decide not to admit an elected candidate because that person does not comply with the requirements for membership or because he or she holds a position incompatible with membership. In this case, the president of Parliament shall notify the Central Voting Bureau of this, without delay.

No Acceptance by the Candidate

Candidates can also not accept their election as a member of Parliament.

In accordance with article 115, if an elected candidate does not accept the election or if, other than in the determination of the result of an election, an existing or upcoming vacant seat must be filled, the chairman of the Central Voting Bureau shall declare, within eight days of being informed of this, in a decision stating the reasons, that the candidate who appears on the same list as the member whose seat has or will become vacant and who is placed highest on that list in the order referred to in article 100, is elected, or if article 93 has been applied, qualifies for election in accordance with the sequence of candidates on the list.

If a candidate who has been declared elected in the place of a candidate who did not accept his or her election also fails to accept election, the name of the first candidate elected is also disregarded, as is the name of every subsequently elected candidate who has not accepted election in further application of the above articles.

In accordance with article 116, disregarded for the purposes of the application of the previous article are candidates:

a. who are deceased;
b. whose vacancies have been filled;
c. who have been declared elected to fill a vacancy, but who have stated in writing pursuant to article 105(2) that they do not accept the election;
d. who are members of Parliament or who have been elected as such, while no decision has yet been reached on their admission; or
e. regarding whom the chairman of the Central Voting Bureau has received a written declaration that they do not wish to be considered for election.

No Compliance with the Requirements and Cease to Be a Member of Parliament

A member of Parliament shall cease to be a member, as soon as it is determined that he or she:

a. does not comply with a membership requirement,

b. holds a position incompatible with membership, or

c. has remained outside the country for a continuous period of more than eight months.

The president of Parliament shall notify the chairman of the Central Voting Bureau of this without delay. Similar notification shall take place if a parliamentary seat falls open through the death of a member.

If a member of Parliament finds himself or herself in one of the situations referred to, that person shall notify the president of Parliament of this, stating the reasons. If such notification is not provided, and the president of Parliament is of the opinion that the member of Parliament is in one of the situations referred to, he or she shall warn the interested party.

If the town of residence and the actual residence of the interested party are not known, the warning shall be recorded in the *National Gazette* of Sint Maarten.

The interested party is free to subject the case to the decision of Parliament within fourteen days, or, if the warning has been published in the *National Gazette*, within three weeks. This term commences either on the day following the dispatch of the warning or on the day following that of its publication in the *National Gazette*. Parliament shall make a decision at the earliest opportunity.

Resignation

A member of Parliament who has been admitted may resign at any time. He or she must notify the president of Parliament of this in writing. The president of Parliament shall notify the government and the chairman of the Central Voting Bureau of the written resignation.

Admittance by Parliament

In accordance with article 122, if Parliament resolves to admit an elected representative, the president of Parliament shall immediately notify:

a. the governor;
b. the chairman of the Central Voting Bureau;
c. the admitted representative.

Within four weeks of the date of mentioned notification, the admitted representative must apply to the governor to take the oath (declaration and solemn affirmation), within the meaning of article 56 of the Constitution of Sint Maarten.

The governor shall then set a date and time at which the oath (declaration and solemn affirmation) shall be taken and shall call up the admitted representative for that purpose. If the admitted representative has not sent in a request to take the oath (declaration and solemn affirmation) within the applicable term, or has not responded to the call to appear to take the oath (declaration and solemn affirmation), the president of Parliament and the chairman of the Central Voting Bureau shall be notified of this without delay by or on behalf of the governor. The vacant position to which the admitted representative was elected is then deemed to have fallen open again on the first day following the expiration of the mentioned term.

Please note that this does not apply regarding admitted persons who are unable, due to physical incapacity, to take the oath (declaration and solemn affirmation), as to be determined by the governor.

Exceptional Situations Based on the Result of the Election

Based on article 93, if the list or lists of candidates contain as many candidates as there are seats to be filled, the Central Voting Bureau shall declare all candidates elected as soon as the term for appeals has expired or, in the event of an appeal, as soon as the Central Voting Bureau has been notified of the decision of the court.

If only one list is submitted, or if only one valid list remains as a result of candidate lists being declared invalid, and this list contains more candidates than the number of seats to be filled, then as soon as the term for appeal has expired, or the Central Voting Bureau has been notified of the decision in appeal, the Central Voting Bureau shall declare as many candidates to be elected as there are seats to be filled.

Furthermore, if no candidate lists have been submitted or the submitted candidate lists contain fewer candidates than there are seats to be filled, as soon as the term for the submission of candidate lists has expired, the Central Voting Bureau shall declare that no one has been elected.

And if, as a result of lists being declared invalid or the scrapping of candidates from lists, no valid list remains, or fewer candidates are included in the valid list(s) (combined) than there are seats to be filled, as soon as the term referred to in paragraph 1 has expired or the Central Voting Bureau has been notified of the decision referred to in that paragraph, the Central Voting Bureau shall declare that no one has been elected.

The Central Voting Bureau shall draw up a procès-verbal of such matters without delay, which will be made available for public inspection at the department of Civil Registry. The provision of the official procès-verbal for public inspection shall be publicized at the same time.

In these cases, new nominations of candidates will take place on the fourteenth day following the date of the official procès-verbal stating that no-one has been elected.

If as a result of the application of the electoral quota, as mentioned in article 95, more seats should be assigned to a list than the number of candidates on the list, the remaining seats shall be assigned to one or more other lists through continuation of the process of application as mentioned in the same article.

Please note that if a candidate has died when the election result is determined, that person's name will not be considered.

Finally, in accordance with article 109, the invalidity of the voting in one or more polling districts or an inaccuracy in the determination of the election result does not prevent the admission of the members whose election cannot have been influenced by the invalidity or inaccuracy and, in the event that voting is invalid, cannot be influenced by the new vote.

CHAPTER 5

Article 59 of the Constitution

The previous regulations concern the regular elections, which are planned every four years in accordance with the term of Parliament, as mentioned in article 46 of the Constitution.

Dissolving the Parliament by National Decree

However, based on article 59 of the Constitution, Parliament may be dissolved at an earlier date by national decree. The mentioned national decree should include the calling for new elections to be held for Parliament with the condition for the newly elected Parliament to meet within three months.

The explanatory memorandum on this article mentions among others the following.

First, that when Parliament is dissolved before the end of its term, the assurance that a newly elected Parliament must convene within a specific term. Therefore, the dissolution needs to be provided in due course and not from the date on which the dissolution decree is issued. This allows Parliament to still complete all sorts of matters, which in this way moreover remains in office in case exceptional circumstances arise. The continuity of the administration is thereby assured.

Second, that the formulation "by national decree" has been chosen, as this better expresses the fact that dissolution falls under ministerial responsibility.

Sint Maarten, since becoming autonomous, on October 10, 2010, has had only one regular election, in the year 2014, and three snap elections in the years 2016 and 2018 and 2020.

When the government dissolved Parliament and called for new elections, it was always a reason for heated discussions— mostly concerning the timing and the authority of the government to do so after losing the majority in Parliament or after a motion of nonconfidence has been presented.

However, the most broad-spread discussion is on the legality of the national decree versus article 59 of the Constitution of Sint Maarten.

The discussion on the authority of the government to dissolve Parliament, after losing the majority in Parliament or after a motion of nonconfidence, will be discussed in the next book on the relationship between Parliament and government.

The Legality of the National Decree Dissolving the Parliament

For now, we will break down the discussions on the legality of the national decree to dissolve Parliament, versus article 59 of the Constitution. In this, the national decree dated September 23, 2019, as amended by the national decree of October 3, 2019, is used as the point of departure.

To understand the discussion on the legality of the national decree, the following needs to be mentioned.

When looking at the procedures for organizing the regular elections, there is a time frame established by law for all the actions by the responsible institutions and government. This is done among other things for transparency but foremost to allow every citizen to exercise his or her passive and or active voting rights. These are considered fundamental human rights. Therefore, not adhering to these time frames, is clearly a violation of these fundamental human rights.

However, when the government has dissolved Parliament based on article 59 of the Constitution, in that same national decree also the date for the first meeting of the newly elected Parliament must be mentioned. In accordance with article 59, this is within three months after the date of the issuing of the national decree. Obviously these three months (after the date of the establishing of the national decree) versus the time frame as established by the Election Ordinance to prepare for elections are not in line with each other.

The result is two scenarios. With the national decree, the three months is maintained, which will result in violation of the fundamental human rights and the passive and active voting rights. If the time frame as established in the Election Ordinance is maintained, the result is a violation of the three-month term as mentioned in the Constitution.

To illustrate, the national decree of September 23, 2019, with reference number LB-19/0642, became active on September 23, 2019. Based on the three months as mentioned in article 59 of the Constitution, Parliament will be dissolved on December 22, 2019, and the newly elected Parliament needs to have its first meeting on December 23, 2019.

In order to achieve this, looking at the dates mentioned above, the postulation of the political parties was scheduled for October 2, 2019.

However, by announcing on September 23 that the postulation date is October 2, a few steps as prescribed by the laws when preparing for elections, were bypassed.

First of all, in accordance with article 23 of the Election Ordinance, only persons with Dutch nationality who are at least eighteen years old and who are registered in the electoral registry on the thirtieth day prior to the date of the nominations, are allowed to participate in the elections.

By establishing by the mentioned national decree that postulation day is on October 2, 2019, the election registry would already have been closed. This means that, for example, high officers of the government who have been temporarily written out of the public registry of Sint Maarten, to register for work in a different country, would not get the opportunity to register and would be denied their right to vote. Also if they planned to run for elections, their right to be on a list would be denied, since you need to be registered in the electoral registry before you can run on a list.

The same can be said for the registering of the political parties. As mentioned in article 3 of the National Ordinance on the registration and finance of political parties, the registration at the Electoral Council needs to be the latest six weeks prior to the nomination date.

Again, by establishing the postulation day in the mentioned national decree on October 2, 2019, the date of the registration of new political parties would be in the past.

Furthermore, based on article 22 of the Election Ordinance, the political parties registered with the Electoral Council may submit a list of candidates to the chairman of the Central Voting Bureau. As is mentioned, this list, prior to the date for the nomination of candidates, shall be published by the chairman of the Central Voting Bureau three weeks prior to the date for the nomination of candidates. This was also not possible due to the date chosen for the postulation date.

The minister of general affairs also has to comply with certain obligations in organizing the elections. One of the relevant actions that should have been taking by the government is the publishing of the colors from which the political parties can choose. The minister of general affairs, at least fourteen days prior to the date of the nominations, should publish the ministerial decree the colors from which the political parties can choose. Obviously, the date of the postulation day as established by the mentioned national decree makes this impossible.

In its letter, the Central Voting Bureau expressed its concern on the situation created.

To remedy the above-mentioned violations, the mentioned national decree dissolving Parliament and calling for snap elections was adjusted by the national decree dated October 3, 2019, with reference number LB-19/0675.

The result, however, is that looking at the date of the coming into effect of the national decree and the first meeting of the newly elected parliament, this period is more than the three months as prescribed by the Constitution.

Namely, the date of becoming valid of the national decree is September 23, 2019, and the first meeting of the newly elected Parliament is on February 10, 2020.

So, it appears there is no regulation on the level of a national ordinance to regulate the snap elections as established by the Constitution. If that is the case, both the Elections Ordinance and the National Ordinance on the registration and finance of the political parties needs to be adjusted.

The Constitution of Sint Maarten

In his letter to the prime minister, in which he presented the signed national decree of October 3, 2019, the governor very explicitly requested attention for the above-mentioned discrepancy between the Constitution and the national ordinances.

The hope is that this discrepancy will be resolved. According to this author, the best way to do this is to make regulations especially for snap elections in the mentioned national ordinances, by adjusting among other things the time frames to be more in line with the Constitution.

Printed in the United States
By Bookmasters